HOW TO GET PAID!

HOW TO GET PAID!

Interviewing with Style

Nan-Lynn Nelson

ISBN-13: 9781523698141
ISBN-10: 1523698144
Library of Congress Control Number: 2016901566
CreateSpace Independent Publishing Platform
North Charleston, South Carolina

Contents

So you're looking for a job. Gainful employment? Nice! Your parents will be very proud of you, and so will we all because that's really all we want: to see the next generation prosper and be in control of their lives. Bravo! I salute and encourage your ambition, because you are our future and I hope this information, I humbly present, will be of great assistance to you.

Whether you've just graduated from college or high school, you've spent a few years working in your family's business, or you were out exploring the world, venturing out into the job market can be a bit daunting without solid preparation.

My name is Nan-Lynn Nelson. I've been a professional actor of stage and screen for over twenty-five years. I have starred on Broadway, featured in television prime-time shows, and in too many commercials to count, from baby diapers to AT&T Communications; "The Bloodhound Gang", on PBS, All My Children, Law and Order, and interviewing, like auditioning, is all an act—one that you have to know how to perform flawlessly.

In my spare time, I have worked with many young people, including the ones who live in my own house, and I have become acutely aware of a particular dilemma you all are being challenged by: public presentation. Don't worry, it's winnable. Your generation has the smarts. I know your generation is the most knowledgeable so far—with your myriad devices spilling tons of information 24-7 into your information-overloaded brains. So, good. Let's figure out how to sort through it all and make a clearing to prepare for some very important and special times in your adult lives. One of those times is interviewing for your first, second, or tenth job.

The following information will consist of a few—not to overload you any more—but very helpful tips, with a dash of good luck, to put you on the right track to success. What is the definition of "luck," you ask? It is "when *preparation* meets *opportunity*." Let's jump right in.

First Things First

DO YOUR DUE DILIGENCE!

1. Don't rely on your good looks and charm to land a gig, job, or employment. Research the company, organization, or individual that you are hoping will hire you, train you,

and pay you money. You're on your electronic device anyway, right? Easy, just look it up.

2. If possible, talk to a person or two who may already work where you are investigating to get the inside scoop. But don't *rely* on their opinion. They may give you a negative report based on *their* experience, but it may not be what you will encounter. Pay attention to the facts: benefit packages, salary ranges, and so forth. Still, trust but verify.

3. By doing your due diligence, you will come to the interview with information about the company to strengthen your chances and of course to impress the interviewer who could be your potential new boss. Make the connection between you and the company's *mission statement*. Oh yeah, *always* know what the company's mission statement is. Google it.

4. Make sure your facts are *facts*, not hearsay, conjecture, or complete and total fairy tales! Research the history. Know something about how the company got started, the CEO, and where the company is headed. Maybe even how *you* can assist with achieving *their* future goals, looking toward the horizon.

5. I know this may go without saying, but I'm saying it anyway: know the industry/business in general and the lingo. Having a knowledge base in the business that you are applying to will make your responses more organic and you more likeable and comfortable. The interview will become a conversation. There will be a flow and a synergy. That's good!

6. Beware of over-talking. You don't want to intimidate the interviewer and come across as a threat or a know-it-all (even if you do know a lot). Psychology plays such a huge part in one-on-one dynamics, and there is always a fine line to walk when trying to impress while avoiding alienation.

7. Have an internal gauge. Your constant talking *may* be fine; just be aware if it isn't. The internal gauge will be helpful with everything you do. It's your intuition. We all have it. Turn it on, and let it assist and guide you.

8. Avoid arrogance, but be confident! You can be assertive by showing your knowledge, establishing a confident tone, and having a polished presentation. Let a little humility be your friend.

9. Have a strong personality, but don't practice your stand-up comedy routine or wear a painted-on tie T-shirt thinking they're going to find it hilarious. They won't.

10. Avoid pranks and negative sarcastic comments, jokes, and so forth.

11. Avoid too much familiarity to the point where the interviewer is uncomfortable. Nerves can do that. Relax. You may find yourself in a situation where you may actually know the interviewer—a family friend, a personal friend, an associate from a previous job. Don't think, "Oh, I got this!" No! Go in just as you would with someone you don't know. After the little familiar greeting niceties, remain professional at all times.

12. Or you may find that the interviewer may be someone of your same ethnic persuasion. *Remain professional!* Don't assume because you *may* have the same societal background that it's time to chill or high five. No! Always take your cues from the interviewer, and remember he or she could just be testing you. It's about business, and the interviewer's job is to find someone who will help the business grow. Not to say you shouldn't have a sense of humor. Again, always have your inner gauge on. And always remain professional!

13. Be honest. A lie will always be found out. If you don't know something, don't say you do. *"I'd like to know more about that"* might be a good response, not simply, *"I 'on't know."* Just kidding, I know you don't really talk like that.

   In show business, actors would often be asked if they had a certain skill: *"Can you roller-skate?" "Jump double Dutch?" "Skydive?" "Speak Swahili?"* The answer was always yes. And then you'd run out and try to learn that skill, so by the time you got that callback or the actual job, you could razzmatazz them a little, *maybe*. Weigh the skill and the risk. Can you learn how to roller-skate, like a pro, in five days? It's a risk but, in my opinion, never a good idea, because if you don't know how to skydive and they push you out of a plane, it *may* be the last risk you ever take.

Honesty speaks to your integrity as an employee and as a person. If there is something negative in your past that might affect your potential for employment, have a prepared positive answer ready. Practice it.

14. *Never ever* speak negatively of past employers, coworkers, or *anyone*. Do not engage in gossip or backbiting of any kind. Remember, it could all be a test. Test or not, don't do it!

Remember, you want to make a good impression by being your confident, capable, and cool self. Your confidence comes by being prepared. This will help calm your nerves and prevent hyperventilation. Even if the unexpected happens, preparedness will help you to stay in control and shine.

2

Facial Expressions

Be aware of your facial expressions. This is something we may not pay much attention to, but sometimes our face is saying something we don't want it to say.

You don't want to look bored or expressionless or like you smell something funky. In an interview, it's important to know what that face of ours might be telegraphing, sometimes unbeknown to us.

Here is a chart and some exercises for your assistance.

Step 1. Look directly into a mirror.
Step 2. Choose any of the expressions in graphic.
Step 3. Hold it for a count of three.
Step 4. Repeat.
Step 5. Now do it without looking in the mirror. Can you envision what your face looks like without seeing?

The purpose is to get to know what your face looks like while it's expressing a variety of emotions.

ADDITIONAL EXERCISES

1. Smile *really, really* hard; hold for a count of three. Let go. Repeat.

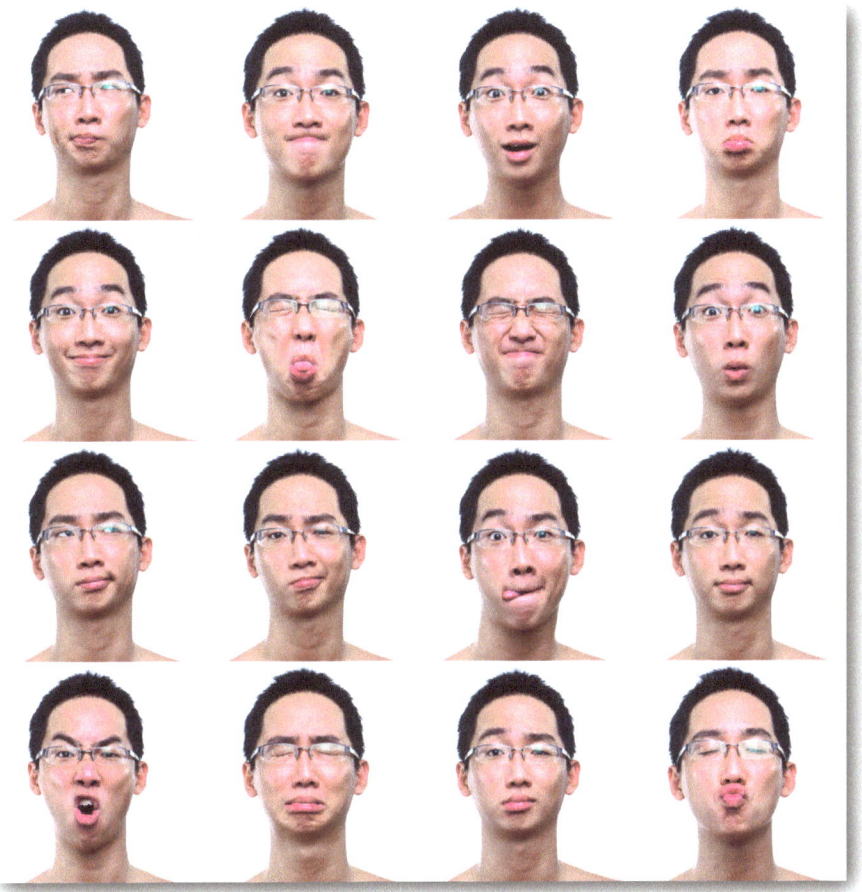

2. Keeping your lips closed, move your mouth as if you are trying to eat a mouthful of peanut butter (or just bread, if you're allergic) and hum. Do it for a count of three. Repeat.

3. Open your eyes and your mouth as wide as you can for a count of three. Let go. Repeat.

4. Same thing as last exercise, except this time, stick out your tongue. Hold for a count of three. Repeat.

We may feel as though what we're thinking is not showing up on our faces, that we're invisible and only visible when we decide to be. It is not true. We can see you, all the time. Know your face.

Make a note of what your "rested" face looks like when you are just listening. To you, it may feel as though you are intensely absorbing everything being said, but to the interviewer, it may appear as though you are bored to tears and about to nod off. Look interested. Practice feeling how your face feels. *Keep it natural*, not scary or creepy. Do the facial exercises.

Our face is the gatekeeper to our emotions. We want to make sure we are showing an "employable" expression.

3

Intern and Volunteer

INTERNSHIPS

These are great to have on your résumé as they show your potential employer how serious you are. Internships offer a wealth of experience, an opportunity for networking, and possibly the advantage of having a mentor. All of these things will assist greatly in a real job.

There are lots of internship opportunities in many locations and industries. *Do your research*. Make sure it is a real internship and not just a business wanting to hire cheap labor. Ask questions: "What are the hours?" "Can you please explain the job description further? Thank you," and so forth.

If you are in school, a real internship may be connected to your school, either high school or college, and will most likely offer credits toward your classes. Check with your guidance counselor or advisors.

The film and television industry may offer internships in the form of production assistance. Often an internship could lead to an actual hire, so always do a good job.

Speaking of doing a good job, I do not mean a "good enough" job but a job that will make you stand out from those who don't have your work ethic. Go above and beyond.

VOLUNTEERING

If you haven't yet, consider finding ways to volunteer. Volunteering is always a plus on anyone's résumé. Seek out opportunities where you could possibly offer a few hours of your time to a community cause, maybe something in your field of interest. This kind of initiative is looked upon very favorably, and in addition, it may also give you some real-life work experience.

Volunteering, like interning, is a great way to get your feet in the door. It puts you in a real-life work environment and builds real skills and self-confidence. It is also a great way to start a network base and a resource to go to for future job references.

Here are a few sites to get you started:

Interning
www.interships.com
www.internationalcommunitydevelopment.org
www.generalassemb.ly/university

www.idealist.org
www.ngocsw.org

Volunteering
www.volunteermatch.org
www.idealist.org
www.volunteennation.org
www.thecommunitycorps.org
www.internationalcommunitydevelopment.org

4

The Devil Is in the Details

This is very important! But what does that mean? Here is my interpretation: it means you must pay attention to every single detail of the tasks required by your job, because if *you* don't, the "devil" *will*, and that will result in making you look *bad*!

An internship is one place where you have the opportunity to pick up on the unwritten nuances that go along with a particular job description. It is a wonderful environment to ask plenty of questions, observe, and be ready to step in and show initiative.

Pay attention to the training, if any is offered. Ask questions during that time to make sure you are understanding just what is expected of you. Don't ask the trainee sitting next to you, because that person doesn't know any more than you do. In addition, by asking a trainee, you risk getting misinformation and looking unreliable when you say, "He (*the trainee*) told me to do that."

When the "devil is in the details," that could also mean you have great ideas, you're able to see the big picture, you have lots of enthusiasm, and you want to jump right into the project. Enthusiasm is great, but be sure you take the time to look at every detail needed to assure a successful outcome.

For example, if you are either an intern or an actual employee and you are responsible for hanging the banner in the room where the very important event will be taking place, it is your job to make sure that the banner gets up there without a hitch. Seems easy enough; however, if you did not pay attention to the weight, length, and height of the banner and if you did not make sure to use the proper secure hanging supplies because you "thought duct tape holds everything," then you were not paying attention or asking the right questions. Now the big important event is here, the room looks great, your boss introduces the guest speaker, and the banner falls on the speaker's head. That means the "devil" was in the details, and had you taken the time to look, you would have seen him and shooed him out of there.

If you don't know, ask. Don't be afraid to ask, no matter how small or simple a question you may think it to be. Ask yourself and your boss. As a voice-over announcer, I used to think I should just know how to pronounce every name I had to say, until I didn't. Once I started asking, "Excuse me, what is the correct pronunciation of this person's name?" I found a level of appreciation I had not noticed before. In addition, I was booked for every gig for years thereafter. There is no such thing as a "stupid" question.

They may not say anything if the banner *doesn't* fall, but they will have a lot to say if it does. All eyes and fingers will be pointing at you, and the devil will be laughing and munching on his popcorn.

Set a high standard for yourself. I tell my own children to always go above and beyond expectations, not to "suck up" but to stay ahead, to learn all you can and have a personal sense of accomplishment.

5

Once you have researched the companies or organizations where you would like to be employed, it is time to start sending out your résumé. Step one for sending out a résumé is the perfect *cover letter*.

This is a letter of introduction. It should say a little something about you but in a dynamic and intriguing way to make the reader want to hear more. You can state briefly your interest in applying for the position and thank them for their consideration. Have some flair, but be succinct, polite, and to the point. If you are doing this via e-mail, of course let them know that a résumé is attached. Check online for assistance in writing the perfect, professional cover letter:

www.cover-letter-now.com
www.gcflearningfree.org
www.quintcareers.com

These are just a few sites to get you on your way. They are also a resource for professional résumé writing. Check them out.

Online seems to be quite acceptable and an often preferred method to send résumés. But look out for the company that may also want a hard copy. Have some available to bring, printed on nice résumé paper, to the interview. There is no shame in following up with a phone call to see if they are in receipt of your "business packet"—your résumé and cover letter and anything else they might request. If you are an actor, you'll also send a picture, black and white or color, 8×10, professionally done, of course. (That will be in my next book.) You may want to inquire if the position has been filled or ask would it be possible to make an appointment at "this time" with the person who answered the phone. Chances are he/she will respond with a no but assure you that someone will get back to you. That gives you every right to follow up a few days later to inquire about that "getting back to you" response you were told the last time you called.

As actors, we master the art of "assertive pursuance" of the role. I should point out, it is a bit risky, as it could turn the folks on the other end of the phone off and give you a reputation of being too pushy or annoying. Again, it's a fine line. Know your comfort level. On the other hand, it could be an admired approach, as long as it is done with tact and grace.

REFERENCES

Have real, honest references. You may be asked to supply both professional and personal letters of reference.

Know the person you are asking to vouch for you. Don't get a reference from someone you just met on the plane or subway. This is where having some volunteer or intern experience comes in handy. It not only gives you real-life work experience but also helps cultivate relationships with people who would be very happy to write something stellar about you and your work performance.

Personal references are important as well. Usually employers will want them to come from family friends, coworkers, or neighbors, not your parents or siblings.

Here are some samples of people who may be good choices for professional character references:

- Former professors
- Former employers
- Teachers
- Camp counselors
- Clergymen and clergywomen
- Supervisors for whom you volunteered

Collecting references is something that you can start doing right away and file until needed. Before you leave your six-week internship, ask for a letter of reference. If you did a good job, they will be happy to oblige. Make sure they are complete with the person's contact information along with name and position, if it's a professional reference.

RÉSUMÉ

Make sure your résumé is polished and accurate. I know folks often fudge (i.e., *lie*) on résumés. It is not worth it. Once it is found out, it could potentially follow you for your entire career. Your *reputation is everything*. Word of mouth travels even faster with all of our modern technology. Yes, there are ways to "enhance," but let's talk about that.

It's all about the *language*. Let's say you write on your résumé that you were an "Activities Coordinator." When asked to "*Talk a little more about that*" by the interviewer, you elaborate by explaining that you worked in your mother's day-care center and were in charge of daily playtime activities for the five-year-olds. So what you wrote is true. There is coordination that is required in such a position. Your mama may not have called it that, but the explanation gives it more clarity and brings it all into focus. It is the truth. The enhancement is in the wording used to describe the position or activity.

Let's face it: gathering information (a.k.a. doing research) to keep five-year-olds engaged and entertained does take skill and preparation and even delegation. Keep it honest. Having that kind of experience is very helpful in building multitasking skills, research skills, creativity, and knowing your "audience."

As the "Activities Coordinator," you had to make choices. How do you make choices? You make them based on the information that you have. What was your information? You had at least six five-year-olds who needed to be engaged in a fun and hopefully educational activity, three times a week, right after nap time. You have to consider the age of your audience, the personalities of your audience, the time this activity is to take place, and the activity's duration. So, should it be a physical activity or something involving working together in pairs, sitting? If so, who should be paired with whom? Are you really going to sit Tarjay with Emma, knowing how much she complains about his humming all the time? No. Your coordinator skills have taken that into consideration, so you will sit Emma with Molly, two girls who always get along and play well together, making your job easier.

Does the day care have to order this activity? If so, do they have sufficient funds in the budget? Did you have to create a budget, based on your favorite "activity supplier," the dollar store?

These are some of the things that as a coordinator you would have to think about in order to have a successful activity period, right after nap time, in your mother's day-care center.

If you say you held an "Activities Coordinator" position and what you actually did was herd a group of cats out of the street once, then that is not an accurate statement. That is what is called a *lie*! Don't do it!

There are plenty of templates in Microsoft Word and other word processors to formulate your own professional-looking résumé. Always start with your most recent job or, for those who have never held an actual job, any relevant activity and education.

You certainly can go on Google and research "résumé format," "résumé content," and so forth. That would be a nice skill to have. There are also professional résumé writers who will be able to set it up for you, ensuring a very polished presentation. Don't forget: first impressions only happen once.

There are many ways to format this very important piece of paper that serves as a personal representation, including adding a photo of yourself, which is an option, and is your choice to make. If you choose to do this, make sure the photo is flattering and professional in jpeg or some other easy-to-transfer electronic file. Résumés are still perfectly acceptable without the photo image. Here are some sites for help with résumé writing:

www.resumehelp.com
www.resume-now.com
www.resumegenius.com
www.livecareer.com/resume-builder

In addition to having a polished résumé, a nice touch is your own personal business card. Some sites, such as www.vistaprint. com, do an amazing job for the right price. They have everything you need to look polished.

Getting Ready: The Night Before

This is so exciting! Time for that cultivated job interview you have prepared so well for. You sent out the résumés with perfectly constructed cover letters. You made the follow-up calls, and now, finally, the company you really wanted has contacted you! Yippee!

Let's start with the night before. *Never* underestimate the night before. It is the perfect time for planning the next day's events.

CHECKLIST

1. You made sure to get that all-important good night's sleep.
2. You did not consume alcohol the night before, avoiding red, puffy eyes or even a headache.
3. You've been drinking plenty of water all week.
4. You remembered to *set your alarm clock.*
5. You also made sure your briefcase or purse is packed with your extra résumés, business cards, mints, ID, a little mirror (to check that nose just before you walk in), and tissues. And don't forget the hand cream (use the nongreasy kind). You don't want to give a greasy handshake.
6. You brought your notes on the company, not to pull out in front of the interviewer but maybe to go over on the ride there, if you're not driving.
7. You have made sure you have the address written in your phone and maybe even marked in your GPS.
8. You at least know what subway/bus to take and what stop to get off. Maybe you've even done a dry run (highly recommended) to get the timing right because you *do not want to be late*.
9. You *do* want to be at least—at the very least—ten minutes early so you can make that run into the ladies'/gents' room to make sure the wind did not totally undo everything you did getting ready.
10. Your entire ensemble is nicely laid out just waiting for the morning sun, from underwear to accessories.

All of this preparation is just to take any additional anxiety out of the equation. No need to allow anxiety to be invited to this party. You are confident and prepared. This will allow you to have a good night's sleep knowing you have everything all set.

Getting Ready: The Day of: Your Personals

The interview begins as soon as you walk off the elevator and into the waiting room to greet the receptionist. Depending on your appearance, it could *end* right there as well! Don't underestimate the power of the appropriate "look."

Gentlemen, if it's an office environment, even if they are known for their "free thinking" and "casual Fridays," err on the side of caution, and wear a suit or at least a nice-fitting blazer jacket, pants, and tie. Designer wear is not necessary, but just make sure it fits and is complementary to your body type and clean and hole free. Borrow from a friend, if necessary.

Ladies, I'm just going to say it: let your words and personality, *not* your "girls," speak for your character and value, if you know what I mean. Once you go down *that* path, be prepared for the fallout that follows, should that actually get you hired.

- In terms of clothing, you may want to explore colors that look best for your skin type and complexion, what colors may make your eyes pop, or what colors complement your hair and skin.
- It may be worth the research to perhaps experiment with different styles that fit your body type. I would stay away from form-fitting dresses unless it is accommodated with a nice, loose-fitting jacket.
- You may want to be trendy, but word to the wise, save that for some other time. You may have a range of conservatism depending on the industry. However, staying closer to the middle range of style will likely be more to your advantage, because it will be *you* they're focusing on, not how trendy your outfit is.
- A nicely tailored pantsuit, with the perfect heel, is classic.
- If your interview is in the actual *fashion industry*, then you most certainly would want to be up on the latest trends and dress appropriately from head to toe, but without looking too studied or going into overkill. As mentioned in the introduction, know your industry. Who is trending right now, what is trending right now, what is your idea of "fashion forward"? Be up on the lingo, the standards,

and the projections. Cite some history and bios of famous designers and so forth.

- *Not for nothin', but*…Don't underestimate the power of the iron! Do not think those wrinkles will fall out all by themselves and not be noticed. It is the kind of subliminal data that the interviewers may not notice immediately but that will definitely play into their decision-making subconscious as the off-putting thing they "couldn't quite put their finger on" for not hiring you.
- Jewelry? Stay away from anything too flashy that may upstage you. You are the star of the interview. Save that for the holiday parties and social outings with your coworkers. Unless it's part of your position to attract business, simple but unique is fine. Jewelry that is complementary to the overall look will definitely speak to your sense of style.

HAIR

Men, this may be a little easier for you depending on the length of hair. Make sure it's clean and neat or stylishly arranged on top of your head, unless of course you're bald, which is also very chic! Be unique, of course, with your dreads, braids, and other styles. But neatness, however you interpret that, should be considered.

Women, in general, give the following some thought:

1. Clean goes without saying, right? Of course.
2. If you have a specific haircut or color that requires more frequent upkeep, make sure your stylist is available the day before to assure the hair is looking great!
3. My African American sisters, who, I must say, are blessed to have a variety of ways to style and wear your hair, make sure
   - the dreads are neat,
   - the weave is tight and undetectable,

- the natural is coiffed and even or styled,
- the braids are flattering and not upstaging you, or
- the relaxed hair is fresh and the edges are smooth.

4. My sisters of maturity and wisdom, thanks for joining us. Gray is fine and quite stunning on some, and if that is your choice, bravo! However, there is no shame in a coloring of the silver locks, if one is so inclined.

MAKEUP

We all want to look our best, and some of us may already have an established routine that we've been rocking for years and no one has objected. However, it may be time to rethink by updating that makeup look you've been wearing since middle school. Most people just don't have the heart to say anything to you, but it is with love that I am saying it might be time to refresh the look.

A very easy approach to this is to simply go to one of those makeup counters at the larger department stores in most major cities. There are always workers dying to practice their makeup craft on any stranger willing to sit, for free. Just know that their goal is to convince you to buy a product.

Research. Find a makeup you really like that works for your skin tone and type. Talk to your girlfriends, and ask what brand they use if it's a look that you like. Let the professional makeup folks assist you in finding the right look for you. Do some research, especially if you have sensitive skin. Find the brand that caters to your special skin needs. Don't underestimate the products of smaller cosmetic companies that may not be in the larger department stores.

1. SADE Skincare and Cosmetics, www.sadeskincare.com, is a business that has been around for years. They offer high-quality natural and organic products, particularly for women of color; however, there is something for everyone.

2. Also Carol's Daughter, www.carolsdaughter.com, has a terrific line of luxurious and natural products, from shampoos and conditioners to moisturizers, for all skin and hair types.

3. Paula's Choice, www.paulaschoice.com, is a site that has lots of products and information on caring for all skin types.

4. Nyraju, www.nyrajuskincare.com, is another natural skincare online company that caters to women of color, but skin is skin, and their products will benefit any skin type.

5. Let's not forget the ever-enduring Avon, www.avon.com. It has a wide selection of everything.

These are just a few companies out there that cater to an urban and suburban market. I am not associated with any of these companies at all and have received no compensation for mentioning them. They have no idea who I am.

Natural makeup would be my suggestion. Sometimes that could be a harder look to achieve than it sounds. Look your best. Choose a style that best flatters you. Remember, this is not party makeup. It's daytime business makeup.

Men, I know women have a bit of an advantage when it comes to makeup. It can really be a secret weapon if applied properly. It evens skin tones, hides breakouts, and helps with an overall enhancement of the natural beauty. But skincare is important for all to look their best.

SKINCARE

Makeup will always look better on well-cared-for skin, so get into a good skin-cleansing and moisturizing habit. This goes for men and women of all ages.

1. Know your skin type.
2. Use scrubs.

3. Drink plenty of water. A nice pH balance in your drinking water is beneficial.
4. Treat yourself to a facial every now and then.
5. Don't forget the importance of proper nutrition and exercise toward good skincare and optimum energy.

Stop with the greasy chips and sweets, please! Don't binge on Häagen-Dazs the weekend before you have the scheduled interview.

As always, research! Do your homework, and find a nutritional regimen that works for you and your lifestyle. Looking good starts on the inside!

8

Teeth! Breath! Underarms Etc!

Again, I would be remiss were I not to bring up this subject, especially with my smokers and coffee-drinking readers. Just follow the *ABCs* of fresh breath: after a good brushing *and* flossing, *A*lways *B*e *C*arrying mints, breath spray, or dissolvable breath sheets, and *not* gum! Do not walk into an interview chewing gum. Thank you.

Don't forget to brush your tongue too! Nab the stink!

Any missing teeth or severely discolored or distractingly crooked teeth may be something you want to address prior to a job interview where appearance is part of the job. If you have to deal personally with the public or clients to make a sale or secure a contract, your smile or lack thereof could make or break the deal.

There are new dental services that can address most aesthetic dental issues in a day. I'm sure financing is available. The methods offered by www.clearchoice.com come to mind. This is not an endorsement. Research!

Plain and simple—don't stink! That's right, I said it! Shower the day of, not just the night before. Perspiration is a natural function of the human body. We all do it; however, when we are nervous, we tend to do it in overdrive. It can become an issue. The stain is unsightly, and the smell can be overwhelming and distracting to both you and the interviewer being subjected to it.

Save the all-natural deodorants for a day at the beach! I'm just saying. I am a big consumer of organic and all-natural products, but when your adrenaline is pumping from nerves while you're sitting in the lobby, waiting to be called in for this important opportunity, you want something that will not turn on you like a jealous understudy waiting in the wings and expose your nervousness. Unless you have been using your natural deodorant for a while and can trust that it will do its job, don't use it on that day. Trust me, I've been there. Use *antiperspirant*. I hate that I'm even saying it, but if that polyester-blend blouse, shirt, or jacket gets hit with that nervous moisture and it's eighty-nine degrees outside, say good-bye to the gig. I'm not saying to use it all the time, it's just that sometimes you may not want to take that chance.

There are brands that are good and gentle like

1. Dove (it comes in a variety of fragrances too),
2. Jack Black Pit Boss Antiperspirant for sensitive skin,
3. Arm & Hammer, and
4. Dry Idea.

Just to name a few that won't cause those of us who are of the more natural persuasion when it comes to cosmetics to freak out. *PS*: I don't endorse any of them personally, just suggesting and pointing you in that direction.

Keep your fragrances low keyed. We don't want to *smell* you coming. Often, people are allergic to perfumes, so please use them sparingly, if you must.

MANI-PEDI AND GROOMING

- Ladies and gentlemen, there are an endless number of places to go in any given city, whether there is a giant mall or just a sidewalk with mini malls, for an affordable manicure and pedicure.
- Eyebrow waxing or threading: If you're getting your eyebrows waxed, always ask for a new, clean stick, not the same one they've been using all week.
- Shaves and haircuts: Always be sure the establishment has licensed practitioners and adheres to health and safety regulations.

- You might think that being well groomed doesn't particularly stand out, but if you *aren't*, it will stick out like a toe in a holey sock!

Just a general comment: "You only have one time to make a first impression!" Make it count!

9

Diction! Articulation! Projection!

OK, so this could be the "make it" or "break it" time. Your speech. You could walk into a room wearing a beautiful, top-notch, nicely pressed, and flawless designer outfit. Color is working, shoes are killing it, the manicure is dope, and the hair and makeup are on point. You open your mouth to speak, and "gobbledygook" comes out, whether it's Ebonics or Appalachian speak, mumbling, or a thick accent from another country or another region. If you cannot be understood, you've just lost that gig. Period!

Don't be too cool for consonants! You have to speak clearly. Pronounce your words completely, using the consonants at the beginning and the end of your words. It's just about communication. If the interviewer is not understanding your words, because you are slurring or your accent is too thick or you're talking too low or just mispronouncing and being inarticulate, your chances of securing the gig just got slim to none. Whether you know what you are talking about or not, when you speak clearly, in a crisp and projecting manner, folks will think you *do* know what you're talking about, and they will want to hear more.

For example, a very common mistake a lot of folks make—whether they are from the inner city of Timbuktu or Appalachia high or low or somewhere in between—is regarding the word "ask," which is a verb; it is an action. It is not a noun. "Ax" is a noun. It is a thing. An "ax" is a chopping instrument for taking down trees or splitting wood. The "x" in "ax" is hit hard at the end, as it should be.

The word "ask" has a very pronounced "s" in between the "a" and the "k," which must be heard in order for the listener to know you are saying "assssssk" and not "ax." Both words have a similar sound at the end with the "k" and the "x" having a hard hit.

If you are saying the word "ask" and have trouble pronouncing the "s," take your time. Say "s" as if you are hissing like a snake, "sssssssssss," then add the "k" sound at the end. Next pronounce the letter "a" with the hissing sound of the "s" and the "k" combined. Practice. See the diction exercise that follows.

Do not underestimate this skill. This will exude a certain confidence that the interviewer will appreciate. Diction is not about "talkin' white," as I have heard some folks refer to it. This section on diction is for *everyone*! It's not black or white; it's just articulation. It is simply about clear, effortless communication of speech, in an arena where there is a particular standard across the board and a skill best to hone. Let it be your calling card. Keep your flavor—it's part of who you are. Just express it precisely

DICTION EXERCISE

1.   Find something to read—magazine, newspaper, cereal box. Read a portion of it out loud, about a paragraph or so.

2.   Now, take a number-two pencil, and hold it lengthwise in front of your mouth. With one hand holding the eraser end and one hand holding the writing end, gently push the pencil back onto your second set of molars. *Gently* bite down on the pencil with your back teeth. Don't break it!

3.   Now, read that same paragraph again, out loud, as if the pencil is *not* in your mouth. Over-enunciate *every single word*! Make sure you hit *every* consonant at the beginning and end of *every* word. Your tongue should feel as though it is getting a real workout. It is a muscle after all. It will be a challenge. Don't give up!

4. Take the pencil out of your mouth (wipe it off with a tissue), and reread that same paragraph out loud. Feel and hear the difference in your diction. If done correctly, the words should swimmingly and smoothly emerge with grace and ease. Repeat often.

5. Keep in mind you don't want to speak like a Shakespearean orator or professional public speaker. The point is to make you aware of how much you are not articulating and correct it. Keep it natural but clear.

6. Record yourself on any kind of recording device, and listen to your voice and articulation. Start training your ear to notice when you are not hitting those consonants.

THICK ACCENTS

I love accents. As an actor, I use them all the time. It becomes part of my characters. Having an accent is great. If you have one, you just have to be able to speak so that the accent does not hinder communication, if that is what the job requires.

So try the following:

1. Listen to talk radio or any news broadcast with the intent of trying to imitate the speakers.

2. Buy a recording device—there is probably one on your phone or computer—and record yourself.

3. Listen to your voice, and see if it is matching up with the way you want it to sound.

4. Use the pencil exercise mentioned above to strengthen the tongue, and get it to do what you want it to do.

5. Continue to read aloud passages from books, magazines, and so forth. Tune your ears to the sound of your voice, and determine if your accent is getting in the way.

I hope you get that having these communication skills will enhance your interviewing-process experience greatly, because you are being heard and understood, no matter who the interviewer is. We, being the "melting pot" that America is, often live in a dual existence: the one we share with our family and friends—the casual, hanging-out self—not thinking about consonants and thick accents so much because our friends understand us, and then there's the professional world, where the standard may be different. Of course you are still yourself, but you will bring a certain awareness to the table if you choose to let consonants be your friend.

10

The Interview

1. OK, so you've made it through the door. What is the first thing you want to do? Look your interviewer directly in the eyes, smile, and give a firm, but not crippling, handshake.

2. No dead-fish handshakes, please! It's creepy and says more about you than any words could. Practice with your friends.

3. Introduce yourself by stating your name clearly. Let the interviewer tell you where to sit.

4. Ladies—yes, I like using the term "ladies"—let's bring respect and empowerment back. Gentlemen, let's bring it back for you too.

5. Having good posture is a very underrated skill, along with diction, which was discussed in the previous chapter. Body language says a lot about a person's confidence and overall self-esteem. Bosses want to be surrounded by people who will not only do a good job but will help make them look good as well.

6. Sit straight up, slightly lean forward perhaps. No slouching. Do not slouch! Sorry, I don't mean to yell, but I have to make sure you hear me. Keep those shoulders relaxed but strong and your back straight.

7. Ladies, might I suggest that you sit with your knees together, or legs crossed, or both knees turned to left or right crossed at the ankles. Be comfortable but always ladylike.

8. Yes, men and women are equal, but that does not mean we are the same. We should celebrate our differences as they only serve to complement and elevate one another. Certainly, ladies, if you want to sit with your legs wide open, with a skirt or pants on, that is completely your choice. I wouldn't recommend it. Choices have consequences, reactions, and responses, so when we make any choice, we should know what possible outcome there could be as a result.

9. Gentlemen, legs should be however you're comfortable, but I would suggest not too wide a gap. Sit cross-legged, if you must.

10. Ladies and gentlemen, we still are a society where there are expectations about distinct male and female behaviors. Whatever is your natural and comfortable way to sit should result in confidence and comfort for you.

BE PREPARED TO ANSWER QUESTIONS

Are you prepared to answer what may seem to be tricky questions? Following are a few questions that will pretty much be asked at most job interviews. Start your thinking engine, and be prepared with good, solid, honest answers that show you can be clear and articulate your thoughts well.

1. Can you tell me a little about yourself?

Do they want you to recite your résumé? I think not. Talking about yourself may seem a bit foreign to most folks, but it's something we all have to get used to in the job-seeking market.

Talk about your interests and accomplishments and how they directly relate to the position. Do it with passion and excitement. Talk about your volunteer experience, where you come from, hobbies, and so forth.

2. Why do you want this job?

This is where your research on the company's history comes in. By sharing that information and, again, connecting it with yourself and your skills, you will keep the conversation going and the interviewer wanting to know more. Be sure to state the position clearly so you know you are both on the same page.

3. What are your strengths and weaknesses?

Ooh, this could be the trickiest of them all. You want to come across as fair and honest about your strengths with a touch of humility. Express your weaknesses with a touch of positive outlook. Striking the balance on both ends is important.

Be specific. Emphasize your communication skills. Talk about your ability to organize and bring people together on both sides of an issue. Have an example to mention. For example, tell the interviewer about that time you were a summer-camp counselor and you were able to organize the best talent show, making sure everyone got a chance to shine. Be specific.

4. Why did you leave your last job?

Again, honesty is the best policy, but so is finesse. Perhaps say something like "I'm looking for something more challenging" or "I'm looking for something more suitable to my skill sets where I can grow and learn."

If you were "let go," or in other words *fired*, be honest! If it was something like "tardiness," let them know, but also express how much you've learned and grown from your mistakes, if in fact you view your firing as your fault. Some folks were "let go" because funding for their contract was not renewed, which is no fault of theirs. Always turn a negative into a positive.

Come with your references and résumé nicely typed out, even if you've already sent them via e-mail. Make sure it is in a nice folder to prevent it from bending. Chances are, you may be interviewing for the interviewer's assistant's job, because he/she forgot to do things like pulling the references you previously sent via e-mail, and so the interviewer may not have a hard copy handy. How cool will you be when you effortlessly whip out your résumé and present it, saying "Not a problem!"?

No matter what, be direct and confident with warmth and friendliness. Keep good eye contact. Smile. Walk into the interview *as if you already have the position*, and through your demeanor and tone, you'll walk away having left a very good impression.

BE PREPARED TO ASSSSK QUESTIONS

Most interviewers will eventually get around to asking, "Do you have any questions for me?" It's best to have at least two questions prepared to ask. One about the company itself: its future, new departments opening up, technology the company uses, and so forth. Then, if it hasn't come up during the interview, well, I know salary is always a little tricky to bring up, but let's face it, it is why we want the job. Simply ask (but you can find your own words), "I understand this is an entry-level position, which I am very excited about. I'm just interested to know the salary range and benefits that come with the position." Fair enough.

Your ability to ask questions and not be stumped by it shows, again, preparedness and confidence. Don't be afraid to really engage in conversation; don't just see yourself as a "question answerer." Let them see how your mind works by being engaging and charming.

11

The Lasting Good-bye

Thank the interviewer for their time, and let them know what a pleasure it was to meet them. Hand them your business card.

Collect your belongings (pocketbook, briefcase) before you stand up.

Give another firm handshake, and say, perhaps, "I hope to hear from you soon" or simply "Good-bye," "It was a pleasure," or "Thank you."

Give yourself anywhere from a day to a week to follow up via e-mail, especially if you felt like things went well. Make sure you have the interviewer's direct e-mail. You might be able to secure that from the receptionist out front.

Congratulations! You did it! You were prepared, and you nailed it. Oftentimes, even if you don't get the job you interviewed for at a particular time, if you leave a good impression with the potential boss, he or she may be inclined to recommend you to a colleague.

Never despair. Every interview is practice for when that perfect opportunity comes along. You could have given a stellar performance in the interview, but unbeknown to you, a niece or nephew was waiting in the wings. As an actor, we interview and audition as part of our profession. We're often told, "We loved you. You were great! But we've decided to go in a different direction."

You cannot let the rejection define who you are. Have confidence that you are a very employable, talented person who will be an asset to any company, organization, or production.

Although I hope I have been conveying this throughout, if not, let me just state clearly: Thorough preparation for not only a job interview, but for all of your life's ambitions, is about developing a good strong work ethic from head to toe and a high standard of professionalism that will make your star shine brighter because you went that extra mile. Be authentic and honest; put your best foot forward. Be as prepared as possible. Relax. Enjoy and learn from each opportunity.

It's just a matter of time until you "book" the job you want. So, as we say in show business, break a leg! (This is the highest form of good luck there is.)

www.ingramcontent.com/pod-product-compliance
Lightning Source LLC
Chambersburg PA
CBHW040918180526
45159CB00002BA/525